HOW TO WAIT

By Karen Kellock Ph.D.

Manual for Superior Men

A complete theory based on Einstein physics,
Political Psychology, Systems Theory
and Archetypal Psychiatry.

FORMULA
All success attraction
All disease obstruction
All recovery elimination

You must fast on all three
OBSTRUCTIONS:
People
Habit
Food

HOW TO WAIT

Time to say goodbye to everything you're known. Your Time Has Come and If they're not with you 100% then good riddance to em. This is your last day down with the masses. Now your life is spectacularly above them all, the joyless. After escaping malicious attacks we rise to the top in victory and abundance. Loners live ten years longer—is it any wonder? A new vista arises after escaping the painful pugnacious matrix with relational lunatics.

BORN TO BE A STAR

THEY SAW THE WORST/GOD SAW THE BEST
ENEMIES YOU GREW UP WITH
EXPECT BIG ATTACKS
WEED FRIENDSHIP GARDEN FOR SNAKES
CONTROL WHO HAS ACCESS
BAD CHARACTERS WON'T HELP YOU
CALL EM OUT, THEY GET ANGRY
THEY EXIT FROM BAD INTENTIONS
THEY LOVEBOMB THEN WANT FAVORS
GOD WANTS YOUR SUCCESS
THE WORLD IS A GROUPIE
LIVING IN A GRAVEYARD
DRAW BOUNDARIES AND THEY LEAVE
YOU CAN NEVER GIVE ENOUGH
THE LONGER YOU'RE INVOLVED
LOVEBOMBING SWEEPS YOU UP IN IT

BORN TO BE A STAR

THEY SAW THE WORST/GOD SAW THE BEST

Your so-called friends and fake family members saw the worst in you but God sees the best too.

Don't you forget when you were cool with these people, even trying to fit in with those losers so evil.

Everyone will come into your life disguised as an angel but rejecting em gets you to the next level.

Those people began ok but switched on you cuz they still want you out here struggling this way.

Improve and you feel weird vibes from people: that's how you know you went to the next level.

ENEMIES YOU GREW UP WITH

It's sad your enemy was one you grew up with. It's sad it took a angel/stranger supporting you forthwith.

Let em hate you cuz they would never push you towards greatness. They are irrelevant to you sis.

You're on your way to your promised land & victory so be careful as the enemy comes in like a flood see.

They'll provoke your spirit by throwing fiery darts but as you grow you're impervious to dark hearts.

You're approaching a new level and that means a new devil so be ready for new attacks also.

EXPECT BIG ATTACKS

BORN TO BE A STAR

Expect a big attack cuz Satan will go in anyone to attack your destiny. If free of sin you'll be protected see.

No weapon formed against you will prosper chosen ones. Remember that always & be happy son.

Weed your friendship garden for snakes. Their energy doesn't seem right/you've had all you can take.

WEED FRIENDSHIP GARDEN FOR SNAKES

Acknowledging you destroys their ego and that's why they never supported you. That's how cruel.

They've been jealous of you chosen one. That's why you never got support you deserved hon'.

When will manipulative scumbags ever learn to touch not God's anointed? Never, so forget it.

They come into your life disguised as supportive angels but you know they're snakes don't ya pals.

In their presence, you feel used and played but you're so kind they take advantage every single time.

CONTROL WHO HAS ACCESS

Careful who you allow easy access to your divine energy. Boundaries: that's the whole thing.

Your kindness and good heart got you into this but let Godly self-esteem get you out and fast sis.

Be very careful hanging out with the wrong people cuz they can manipulate you out of money too.

When you finally wake up with discernment you see these people are just users & abusers man.

BORN TO BE A STAR

And guess what genius, that's why you have anxiety and can't sleep. They're wolves, you're sheep.

That's why you have depression: emotional abuse--DAMAGE. Use your brains to better manage.

BAD CHARACTERS WON'T HELP YOU

When you need these bad characters the most they'll jump ship. Count on it, reject em/take my tip.

But when they go through tough situations we stand our ground and support em. Be sick of this hon'.

The chosens always end up getting the short end of the stick as their kindness ruins them quick.

Throw all their sweet talking out the door. "Don't tell me nothin, you gotta show me" is your new roar.

They cling onto you for a reason: they know you're nice, a "yes" person but it's a setup for treason.

They know you're nice and will use your kindness to get what they want from you [it's obvious too].

CALL EM OUT, THEY GET ANGRY

When you call em out on their mind games they get mad, citing all they've done for you as facts.

How come there's never any reciprocity? Because the manipulating scumbags are USING YOU see?

They come disguised as your family, friends and narcissist ex-lovers and they're all bummers.

They're your friends from childhood or co-workers: you'd be surprised all your frenemy abusers.

BORN TO BE A STAR

I finally put my foot down: no one could use my kindness as weakness and they were gone sis.

While using you they're breaking your mind. You don't dare call em up for what they're doing, aye.

THEY EXIT FROM BAD INTENTIONS

They come into your life and then leave so fast--why? They had bad intentions and motives, aye.

We chosens wanna see everybody win, until they cross us. That has to be our slogan friend, a promise.

We genuinely wanna see everyone happy with no bad intentions. So why put up with bad person?

We don't wanna use anyone, it's you pour into me and I pour into you but that's a lost concept hon.

Have they ever apologized to you? No they just guilt trip you more, that's how you know they're bad Sue.

True apologizers are willing to change but if they never even apologized or admitted wrong, go away.

If you're waiting for an apology it's not gonna come so you need to be ready to quit and be done.

THEY LOVEBOMB THEN WANT FAVORS

First they lovebomb you then ask for favors like invading your privacy with their friends or whatever.

The minute they get a foot in your door they feel the power. They move right in asking for favors.

You gotta. be so careful who you kindly let in because before you know it they bring all their friends.

BORN TO BE A STAR

The devil [in them] seeks who he can devour. It's spiritual wickedness in high places thru whomever.

You don't know if they have the love of Christ in them. Don't let one you know bring their friends.

People will manipulate you ["I love you"] just to get things outa you and even your body too.

God's right there on your shoulder saying "don't do it, I want to protect you". Hear this & stay apart Sue.

GOD WANTS YOUR SUCCESS

God wants you to have life more abundantly but with users flooding in you'll lose precious privacy.

As one who's overcome horrible things I see: there's nothing more important than privacy.

The social generation always wants to bring friends. It's like they can't relate one to one without em.

To me and my family solitude is HEAVEN. Not having anyone else around so we can enjoy the moment.

But the world doesn't think that way. Most are lonely & bored so being social is at the core [go away!].

THE WORLD IS A GROUPIE

My generation was about the INDIVIDUAL. You come alone so I can get to know only you, that's all.

The nerve of someone once they get in your home bringing their friends gripes me as cold.

We invited her to stay at our estate. She asked if her friends could stay then I wanted her to go away!

BORN TO BE A STAR

People have no respect for privacy cuz they're so used to the social generation where no one's free.

If they haven't experienced the BLISS of solitude they're just naturally rude bringing in their people too.

LIVING IN A GRAVEYARD

We're all a composite of our forebearer's neurosis, our own history and the creeps we knew see.

Becoming whole/cosmic is getting free and clear of this history of the walking dead or graves instead.

Not only are we living in a tomb we recreat the whole mess in our guests or things we tolerated in the past

These reduplications of history and generational curses keep us not ourselves, stuck in neuroses.

One of the most powerful tools you can ever waste is the mind and people will take it from you, aye.

Adapting to people has no small effect. It takes energy and the mind warps easily, I can attest to that.

Ask God to reveal who manipulated or gaslit you. You'll get so very good at detecting it yourself too.

One gets married and fights with new partner thinking it's his ex: we're all owned by the past.

DRAW BOUNDARIES AND THEY LEAVE

The relationship ends when you draw boundaries, cuz they can't do what they must do wee.

The narcissist doesn't remember that you saved her, she only sees that you have more than her.

BORN TO BE A STAR

The narcissist wants you to continue giving to her while encroaching on you constantly as a sucker.

She lives rent free in half your house then instead of being grateful she wants the rest of it now.

You save her from homelessness but instead of being grateful she wants your entire home sis.

That's where their false reality/delusional system is. You're just a dog with a bone they want sis.

YOU CAN NEVER GIVE ENOUGH

It doesn't matter how much they have/you've given them, they want the rest of the pie, amen.

The narc will tell you they don't play games or manipulate but they do it all, it's ingrained.

They do all that gaslighting stuff times ten but can't see it. They're entitled that's all they know, it's basic.

They're so incorrigible researchers say it's the construction of their brain cuz they never change.

She wanted more, I gave her more. That wasn't enough until she had everything and still she implored.

It's like two dogs with a bone. It doesn't matter if one saved the other, it's gonna be a fight that's all.

THE LONGER YOU'RE INVOLVED

The longer your involved the more danger. Cut your losses and forget em quick or it's a bummer.

It lovebombing and FAMILY-bombing: "we're a family, you mean everything to me" but it's all bull see.

BORN TO BE A STAR

They can't justify their own actions and usually won't even try. Stay two steps ahead or bid goodbye.

The lovebomb becomes exciting quickly, esp if you've been alone--but narc abuse follows it you know.

LOVEBOMBING SWEEPS YOU UP IN IT

You've been lonely for so long so the lovebomb sweeps you off your feet. Then the discard kills you see.

They're even jealous you're capable of changing their life. No gratitude except lovebombing, a lie.

You were born a star, destined for greatness. But only if you put the past behind you can you get this.

Hard work beats talent when talent don't wanna work no more. Keep goin' man, soon you'll be a star.

You may be talented and gifted but do you have the work ethic? Genius without success is tragic.

You may be talented but do you have that dog in you, that resilience, that do-it-now power too?

The hardest version of yourself is the BEST version every single day. No more ups and downs ok.

Stop being in such a rush to your destination and enjoy your life journey. It's really the whole thing see.

When they ask you how you did it, say it was ONLY by the grace of God cuz that's the truth isn't it.

Don't be afraid to say you were born to be a star but it took work, diligence and fighting a spiritual war.

THE CHOSEN MUST RELOCATE

THEY TARGET BUT GOD GUIDES
THEY'RE ATTRACTED TO THE SHINE
GOTTA SHUT THE BLINDS
THEY KNOW YOU'RE PECULIAR
THE MISERABLE WANT YOU KILLED
YOU MEET EM THEN HATE EM
LEAVE EM TO THEIR FATE
THEY WON'T DO IT
MAKING YOURSELF DO THINGS
CHAMPIONS ARE SELECTIVE
IF IT DIDN'T KILL YOU, ONLY STRONGER
YOU HEALED CHILDHOOD TRAUMA
GOTTA GO THRU IT TO GET TO IT
GOING TO HIGHER GROUND
FROM PIT TO PALACE
THE DREAM KILLERS
YOU LOOK LIKE GENERATIONAL WEALTH
DO ANYTHING TO MOVE
YOU'LL LOVE YOUR NEW HOME

THE CHOSEN MUST RELOCATE

THEY TARGET BUT GOD GUIDES

They target you but God guides you. That's why you say "order my steps Lord": to avoid the mind screw.

You are LED by the holy spirit and the gang stalkers are led by demonic spirits: that's how to see it.

They are led by dark music and worship false idols. They are blinded by the traditions of men too.

Anything you listen to/watch you'll be full of. So don't wonder why the gang stalkers are rearing up.

Gang stalkers are constantly following you cuz they're led by Satan but attracted to light too.

THEY'RE ATTRACTED TO THE SHINE

They're attracted to anything that shines and you are like a light bulb oh chosen friend of mine.

Anything that glitters, anything of God they'll try to destroy it. It's Satan's world vs. the anointed.

The devil comes to steal, kill and destroy. Those aren't empty words so be on guard putting God first.

Watch what you wear, like jewelry. You don't need to show off chosen one, it attracts thieves see.

God says He chose you, giving the anointing. You are the light regardless of jewelry glittering.

People gang stalk you because they know you do better by yourself. They can't stand it and are jealous.

17

You gotta be [1] strong to be alone and [2] watchful over all your surroundings as the encroach so.

GOTTA SHUT THE BLINDS

I had to have all the blinds shut and the lights off so they wouldn't know I was home: it was rough.

It was a small liberal town and they are the worst. Being so social if you refuse so they target you know.

When in large groups with all eyes on you, move around. Cuz God's gonna take you higher and renowned.

Keep moving around so you'll finally meet people who are just like you. Better days are coming too!

Better opportunities and people are coming and you don't have time to stoop to losers staring.

THEY KNOW YOU'RE PECULIAR

They know you're a peculiar person, wonderfully and beautifully made like God so own it son.

Miserable unhappy people will suck the life right outa you friends. You gotta guard your energy, amen.

Their misery will strip you of everything that is you. They will sabotage everything you have Sue.

They will diminish everything because that is who they are. It's impossible to be around em as a star.

Unhappy people have all sorts of issues so it's impossible: they'll find a way to wreck it all.

These people are dangerous. They will dig & dig til they find a way to bring you down on purpose.

You must distance yourself from people and just focus on you for it's a helluva thing to deal with Sue.

Thus chosens don't deal with many people in the first place. It's a nightmare and they'll be disgraced.

Few have it together. My favorites are those who do & are self-aware. They know what they're doing, hear?

THE MISERABLE WANT YOU KILLED

The miserable will get you killed and drag you straight down to hell with them, guaranteed/sealed.

They don't wanna hear anything true about them cuz it's too much. They don't wanna do it as such.

Test it and you'll see it's true. They can't have a regular conversation without hijacking it Sue.

As a psychologist I know what unhealthy people can do to healthy people and thus I say: stay away.

Never underestimate the dire effects of being around unhealthy people. You'll die from their evil.

Unhappy people are the most stubborn and arrogant. They're dumb but don't know it: avoid it.

They will never change. They won't put in work needing to be done so there's no improvements hon'.

YOU MEET EM THEN HATE EM

You meet someone at a gym and feel it's ok then slowly or suddenly you see who they are, dismayed.

Even being around these people will have a deep effect on your life. Don't minimize the spirit of strife.

The sooner you realize this the sooner you'll be on your way. You can waste years/decades in chaos ok.

They won't do what they should and will always resort to their ways. Get out while you can ok?

They're not even remotely close to your level so don't let your magnanimous spirit tolerate the devil.

They have their fate, their time will come. But in the meanwhile what happens to you with these bums?

LEAVE EM TO THEIR FATE

Their fate is their fate and it's sad but it's gonna happen and you warned them: there will be no heaven.

They're traumatized and it's deep. Thus they will never change and existence will be very painful see.

We were traumatized but did everything to heal. We did the work but truthfully/sadly they never will.

It's about finding the solution & doing it. But they won't: miserable people will stay stuck, believe it.

They always resort to who they are and will never work hard enough to get outa that: to be a star.

They know they have issues and they say they'll do it but never will. The don't do it and go to hell.

THEY WON'T DO IT

They don't do it, they don't have to do it. They get arrogant about it & you're in trouble to push it.

They will always prefer a fantasy world to buckling down like you boys & girls. They're lost, not you.

Nothing is ever going to change. NOTHING, nothing. Face that and be on your way to destiny.

They dream of something big coming to change their life but it never will and they'll never work at all.

Change takes hard work, commitment and discipline. Those are the big three that stumps most men.

MAKING YOURSELF DO THINGS

Making yourself do things and not caring that it's gonna be a challenge is the mark of the champions.

Saying: "I have a lot of work ahead of me and I WILL do it and I WILL win": that is the true champion.

The champion devotes every day of life to it in total devotion. That's how it is to get what you want son.

It should feel like a miserable time when you're not accomplishing on it. Every single day, push it.

You have to be damaged, toxic and a weirdo to even fit into society. You're fully accepted, best ever see.

When you choose to do better with your life they'll team against you. It's insane to find this out too.

The champion spends half his life on his talents and the other half managing people coming against it.

CHAMPIONS ARE SELECTIVE

The champion is selective of who he's around and shuts out most of the world, that's what I've found.

Your energy is so powerful--being one with God--your silence is deadly. They can't stand this see.

No one messes with one who hit rock bottom already and wrestled to the mountaintop buddy.

Making it back from rock bottom makes you a powerhouse that cannot be defined, ouch.

IF IT DIDN'T KILL YOU, ONLY STRONGER

Anything that didn't kill us made us stronger, in the physical and the spiritual. We proudly walk tall.

Overcoming things like that makes you know who you are. From what you've overcome you're a star.

After all that you're still shining and smiling. They never see you down now, so strong from overcoming.

Even when you're broke you have your chin up. You've learned the ropes from the past screw ups.

People are intimidated by your posture, the way you walk and speak but mostly your control see.

You gotta stay vigilant just in case, cuz Satan's roaming around seeking to target God's kids.

Energy vampires seek to destroy knowing your spirit belongs to God: they attack thru your flaws.

What you've been thru made you powerful and humble. No one can compete with that, even know it alls.

YOU HEALED CHILDHOOD TRAUMA

You healed from childhood trauma while they stayed sick. You've got class but they're still hicks.

You can never get to where God is taing you while stuck in a toxic environment. Gotta get up out of it!

They're plottin' and plannin' how to destroy you because you're out here winnin' and shinin'.

In the toxic environment they'll kill you over status. They'll lie on you just to get what you possess.

God may keep you safe in the toxic place but it's gonna be hard and you may still end in disgrace.

God will wake you up from sleep to let you know someone's stealing from you. Awake or be screwed.

The gang stalkers don't know what you've been thru to get to this day. You're a shining light anyway.

GOTTA GO THRU IT TO GET TO IT

You gotta go thru it in order to get to it. So buckle up and bare it with God helping you in the face of it.

God will take every stumbling block & fiery dart coming your way but it's still gonna hurt if you stay.

God will smash everything coming against your breakthrough but there's things you still gotta do.

It was a spiritual battle for me to move outa the toxic environment. It was a major disentanglement.

If you're around someone who's jealous of you or nosy ass neighbors life can be hell, a real bummer.

Don't befriend people in your environment. Go to where you need to be, pressing towards the mark.

GOING TO HIGHER GROUND

You need to plant your feet on higher ground so what do you care about people in your hometown?

That's when I realized I was a chosen one: when my own people wouldn't accept me in my hometown.

Even when I had the decency to go back & help em up they still showed me who their true colors, yup.

Once in your new home you'll see why God had to relocate you. It's a springboard to a heavenly crew.

FROM PIT TO PALACE

You will now have made it from the pit to the palace. After everything overcome you deserve this.

You've been thru the fiery furnace and came out unburned. You're elegant after everything learned.

That great person living with you stole from you and went thru your mail. People are a giant fail.

Just to get to your next level you had to bite your tongue. The devil wants you to lash out wrong.

Satan wants you to revert to bad version, what you used to be. Cussing people out keeps you unfree.

It's hard holding your tongue/keeping your peace til you see the devil wants to destroy you, so please.

Those jealous of you don't have the same anointing & are not on the same level so escape their hell.

THE DREAM KILLERS

Those dream killers lied on you behind you back to make themselves look good, understood?

Just like me you have to go thru the storms of life to get to the sunshine. The rain before the sun, aye.

Those people were low vibrational snakes. That was your environment but it's also what it takes.

They're demonic. God said He'd do anything to protect you but pack your bags or it can be tragic.

Pack your bags and get outa your family house cuz they're jealous and trying to destroy you sis.

The first time God woke me up was when I found a housemate going thru my wallet like a lunatic.

YOU LOOK LIKE GENERATIONAL WEALTH

Your aura bespeaks generational wealth. Even if you drive a bucket they want it: society is hell.

Even if you wear hand me downs they want it. It's all cuz you the anointed are the one wearing it.

You can be wearing a trash bag and you still look better than them. They just hate you for your anointin'.

They recognize the amazing anointing but just hate the fact that its you who's carrying it darling.

You could wear a plastic bag on the top of your head and you'd still look far better than them.

Your aura speaks generational wealth like a dynasty. It's monumental and an amazing thing to see.

DO ANYTHING TO MOVE

You may have to live in a storage room before God puts you in your big ol' house but do it for success.

In a toxic place they can't stand you being anointed & wanting to give, they don't want you to live.

God will take you through it but will also pull you out of it. Don't ever be afraid to not put up with it.

God said if you didn't put Him first you'd stay in that toxic ass environment for life & what a curse!

You have greatness in you and you livin' in the hood still? That's a life without God and it's hell.

You gotta move, get your own place and go to people who will love and appreciate you as the Ace.

You'll have new people who will have your back and approach you with the love of Christ, a fact!

YOU'LL LOVE YOUR NEW HOME

I love my new environment and my neighbors. They pray for me and I for them for heavenly favors.

Regardless that some can't stand you they still need you at the palace and that's your new address.

Go where you're celebrated not tolerated. That's always the two contrasts, that's the truth of it.

In the toxic environment they feel you need them so they just tolerate you: they're not your friends.

Thinking you need them they can't tolerate it when you do better, that's the sure sign of a chosen one.

When people have more than you and you STILL shine bright like a diamond anointed, they hate it.

When people have more than you yet STILL jealous of you that's how you know you're chosen.

The minute you move from the pit to your new mansion you get first class treatment, I promise you kid.

THE BLOODY NERVE

IN OUR STREAM, NO COMPETITION
MUD: A POVERTY OF IDEATION
BE A LEGEND TO YOURSELF
GRIEVING LOST HOPE
NEVER VENT EMOTIONS PUBLICLY
CRYING OVER IMMATURE GUYS
THE LITTLE GIRL THING
BE A LADY OF SUBSTANCE
UNDERTOW TO QUEEN CONSCIOUSNESS
POWERFUL OLDER WOMEN
DAM DROP INS
VIOLENCE STAYS IN THE SOUL
PULLING DOWN STRONGHOLDS
A SICK SYSTEM USES OUTSIDERS
HEADACHES AND CONFLICT
LOOKING BACK
SECRET COALITIONS IN SYSTEMS
BROKEN QUEEN CONSCIOUSNESS
TOXICITY TURNS BACK
THE ELITE MYSTICS
PUSH EM TO THE EDGE
CHASING WOMEN AND SEX, REJECTION
WOMEN AND REJECTION
CHASING WOMEN ARE NOT VIRTUOUS
DON'T CHASE: BE VIRTUOUS
FINISH ASSIGNMENT, BREAK IN CLOUDS
DEMS LIKE DRUNKEN SAILORS
WEAK LEADERS OR HITLER
AS THE LYMPH CLEANS OUT
NUTRITION'S AN EXCUSE TO EAT
GREAT NEWS FOR THE SMART
WAIT FOR THE PEARL

HOW TO WAIT

HAPPY LIFE FREE OF STRIFE
HOW TO WAIT: DISENTRENCH FROM THE DIS
EXTREME VACILLATIONS
WE WANT NO SOUL TIES
MALIGNANT NARCISSISM
WHEN I THINK OF YOU
PROJECTION OF JEALOUSY
SMALL TOWN SMOTHERING
ETERNAL: TRANSCENDING PEOPLE
UNRESOLVED TRAUMAS TO THE CORE
WEAK LEADERS HAVE ARMIES
ECCENTRICS LIVE TEN YEARS LONGER
SINISTER PEOPLE LIE, CHEAT, STEAL
MONKEYS ARE TWO FACED
TOXIC, SINISTER, DEMONIC PEOPLE
SECONDARY MONKEYS: LAWYERS
GOD'S TIMING
LIFE IS BRAND NEW EACH MORNING
GOD GAVE YOU IDEAS AND HE HAS THE LINK
SOLITUDE LOVERS ARE "HATERS"
MUST SOAR LIKE THE EAGLES
NOTHING'S HAPPENING SO YOU'LL RELY ON GOD
DESTINY MOMENTS ARE LINED UP
WE'VE BECOME CULTURALLY INSANE
THEY STATE THE OBVIOUS
MUST BUILD BACK UP
SEPARATE PROTECTED SOLITUDE
FLYING MONKEY HATRED [BAD ASSOCATIONS]

HOW TO WAIT

HARD LESSONS: NEVER AGAIN
COUNT ON GOD'S FAVOR
KK THOUGHTS WHILE WAITING
CREEPED OUT BY MY GENERATION
DEGENERATION OF BLOODLINES
DUMB WOMEN AND TRUMP-HATRED
HIX POLITIX
SUCCESS MAKES A HUGE MESS
PEOPLE WORSHIP REPLACES GOD
HUGGIN' AND KISSIN' IS SICKENIN'
WORDS CREATED WORLD: WATCH 'EM GIRLS
I DON'T WANNA GO ANYWHERE
SO YOU SCREWED UP, SO WHAT
LOOKING BACK BRINGS PANIC, DON'T DO IT
CONTACT = CONQUEST
GOD WANTS TO BRING YOU OUT!
GOING BACK TO THE PITS
YOUR WEAKNESS ATTRACTED EM
PEOPLE CAN BE DOWNERS
OBESITY AND DEATH FROM WALMART'S BAKERY
FAST TO BE HAPPY IN AN AGEIST SOCIETY
CLOSE YOUR BORDERS FOR SUCCESS
INVADED, OR DID YA LET EM ALL IN?
CONTAGION OF LUNACY
CURE FOR LOSERS: BECOME FASTERS
EATING BECOMES IRRELEANT CHORE
SOME FRUIT AND A BOWL OF RICE A DAY
THE END THOUGHTS

THE BLOODY NERVE

While you respond from the spirit--God's and your own--they respond to each other/crazy norm.

When its your own sister destroying your reputation you understand sibling abuse in sad recognition.

When siblings are jealous there's nothing they won't do miss. You'd better mature before it hits.

I'm sorry for what I said, a faux paus. Not fully healed it was an autonomism from the unconscious.

God promised completion, you won't wait forever. There's a date to the second so persevere.

Helen Copley owned 31 newspapers so can't be all wrong: tiny queens ruled, read Silver Dons.

God uses the flawed: A generation of pit vipers and evil children but even so God can use em.

It's an INNER journey, not an outer one. Get offa this social thing the public schools drummed in.

IN OUR STREAM, NO COMPETITION

No competition: I developed rare arts/techniques to perfection bringing insults and rejection.

Those people in the bleak past were just archetypes and old now, they may be gone as dust blows.

We swim in muddy waters like we don't know any better. Forgive thyself and enter the future.

THE BLOODY NERVE

You have to work hard to keep things nice since the default setting now is disorder and vice.

You didn't appreciate me so to hell with thee, that's all I gotta say after this charade and treachery.

There IS no competition cuz we're in our own stream: at our own steam pressure/energy level see.

There's no one who can compete with me cuz no one can do what I do see: stop this anxiety.

At last, you can enjoy a sunset, be excited when you get up, fully charged ready to conquer it.

MUD: A POVERTY OF IDEATION

You've been living in mud, a poverty of ideation and boring as hell cuz you didn't know what's up.

Humans adapt to their environment. If it's disordered, crazy or violent they too get screwed up.

Since when does popularity indicate quality? The mediocre gets likes from the peanut gallery.

Since when is "social connectedness" a true indication of a great musician, scientist, or artist?

Your light cannot be hid under a bushel forever. Wait on God for there is an exact minute of favor.

BE A LEGEND TO YOURSELF

Be a legend not just to self but all who knew what you went thru before maturity as magic elf.

It is looking out the window that is most profitable so don't let em judge when you stop it all.

Captivity and made to conform to thee is the worst possible notion I could ever have see.

He won't take the trash/sweep the leaves but hasn't he always solved your problems sweetie?

Tho' it hurts seen as scum recall with God all things resolve and you're on top--you've won.

Broken consciousness says you're too old, can't get better, must tolerate this situation forever.

Pull back from this thing, cut this thing off and grieve the disappointment: work it through/sob.

GRIEVING LOST HOPE

You are grieving lost hope. But it got you to where you are today: I wrote over 100 psych books.

You had hope in this thing, that it would be what you desired it to be for eternal happy loving.

If it turned out to be a lie, you gotta grieve it. There's no getting around it, face it then forget it.

You grieve it to finalize in mind that it's dead. Sob, cry, pray to God then start a new life instead.

You grieve, then the funeral. Unrelenting disappointment left you heartsick but that's gone now.

It's never gonna happen: finalize in mind [that this is dead] so your future opens just like God said.

While grieving lost hopes anchor yourself in dignity. This is most important or it's the end of thee.

You gotta know who you are/not fall to new lows. Begging, crawling back: be more dignified than that.

Anchor yourself in dignity and be the pretty little lady who God, angels and parents saw you to be.

NEVER VENT EMOTIONS PUBLICLY

Never publicly vent your emotion. Don't be all over facebook showing weakness as a victim.

Venting publicly is just inviting more predators to come into your life so caveat: keep it private.

Suddenly you're whimpering like a little girl, hoping for help or pity but that will never end well.

I heard my voice go into my little girl talk, hoping this guy would finally let up but sadly he didn't.

If he says you're too old, accept a new station with you in the dominant position as elder wisdom.

Stop talking like a little girl to compete with teenage nobodies. Take a leader position and see.

Stand up, be an attractive strong lady, an elder if need be. This is so much more stunning/godly.

When a little girl crying worked, bringing help and pity from good guys or jerks, but no more girl.

Your lovesickness comes from inner bitterness from deferred hopes that rope you in more.

Grow up then put young girls down but until you do, it's an embarrassing Baby Jane Syndrome.

CRYING OVER IMMATURE GUYS

Crying, crying, crying: can't you see it's early trauma repeating itself in this loser/immature guy?

THE BLOODY NERVE

I talk to women daily and I commiserate. I remember the nights wanting to die, at a young age.

I had a fear in the gut--the solar plexus--that was only relieved by food, booze or that gigolo too.

The funeral has been had, this situation is dead, but now you gotta bury it psychologically instead.

Your face is a carving of destiny now, a wisdom showing all around in a patina from loss overcome.

Imagine the guy in twenty years, as aging narcissism becomes desperation-- his tactics don't work.

You can have success in your work but if not mature the weakness will raise its ugly head for sure.

I felt kicked in the gut from secret coalitions and rep destroying gossipings, calling on God daily.

THE LITTLE GIRL THING

You must talk like a little girl so he won't hurt you, treat you like a tool or so he'll return to normal.

I recall it so well: slipping into my little girl bag. You reach a point where it's an ugly tactic.

It's living in delusion that hurts, not the truth. Betrayal is a shock but you'll come out better too.

A fifty year old woman talking like a little girl, what a freak. Gotta grow beyond Baby Jane see.

Just be a single elder queen for awhile. Self-respect is worlds ahead of where you've been gal.

You slipped into your little girl bag and sobbed as you begged. Learn to laugh at something this sad.

If you can let this cad go it'll be your season. Prepare for godly showers cuz you overcame him.

It was horrible being on the begging end, admit it. Just cuz you weren't up to snuff in his matrix.

It's disgusting how the little girl act manipulated men, something you also must face and amend.

BE A LADY OF SUBSTANCE

You gotta go full force in self-expression now, a lady of substance not that damned/silly little girl.

He went for younger women, increasingly putting you in desperation. See his immaturity/grow beyond.

I've been there, done all this and I can tell you Miss: it's hell on earth living in this sorry/sad matrix.

Having overcome jerks now you're only happy when you work. Then, finally, you live to enjoy leisure.

Cuz sis was older all believed her but two sisters is Cinderella wanting a prince to rescue her.

The worst is when a queen gives in sexually [again] when he doesn't even deserve a conversation.

Decreased self-esteem from systems so mean: it's a process, study it and don't go back again.

UNDERTOW TO QUEEN CONSCIOUSNESS

It's an undertow to queen consciousness, she uses him to counter this, the system becomes ridiculous.

Ignore gossip, you and God know the truth and that stands: a Christian shall not be condemned.

THE BLOODY NERVE

What they did to bring you down was wrong man--and that fact will be known by the whole clan.

What they said about you was horrible. Calumny like that recalls the case of Justice Thomas.

You practice the principals, you get hurt, it's discussed, you try it again eventually able to trust.

POWERFUL OLDER WOMEN

A beautiful woman without discretion is like a gold ring in a pig's snout--yah tell me about it.

Nothing more attractive than an older woman who doesn't fear aging but just takes dominion.

Education, experience, wisdom, probably property and knows who she is today as a matriarchy.

So go away little boys and have your tarts with whom you've little in common but the dark arts.

The narcissist tells who he is in so many obvious words but you're too heartsick to see it girls.

He tells you he's a player: he brags about it everywhere but you think you can change the little dear.

He'll always be the same just not successful at the game but finally need you for a place to stay.

Men are warped, women are warped. We swim in muddy waters and both had poor character.

Daily Writer Routine: Write until you can't write anymore then you're off for afternoon/evening.

Our worries are slight compared to what people went thru in WWII. Have perspective/not just you.

THE BLOODY NERVE

People were taken from their homes to horrible camps and killed. My God girl you have it so good.

Now stand up and get ready to attract a real man soon. For this you gotta make room/rid the goon.

If they don't get right to it my mind wonders. So much superfluity and non-essentiality: bores.

They dither and dither and half the day's gone. I'm sick of guests or being a guest, that's all done.

They say "men are evolving fast" cuz they're crying more in the movies not less and what a disgrace.

Men are going to come around asking for her hand cuz she's Ms. Social Charm, integrating a man.

Ever reading but never coming to the truth. Learn what you can then look out window, fitting it all in.

DAM DROP INS

I get involved in projects and hate interruption. About you coming unannounced, don't do it again.

They drop in cuz they're bored/lonely and it drives you crazy. Get a fence or learn assertion quickly.

You start a project or study and they drop in--more irritating surprises. The elite can't stand this.

If you were invaded in your home that violence is still in your soul and PTSD is real/none to console.

You don't have time to suffer drop-ins who aren't busy so they friggin' drive you crazy: drop em.

It's a system: your aura of neuroses, weakness and boundarilessness and their greedy creepiness.

THE BLOODY NERVE

When at liberal university I drove all the way home every Friday just to escape the bloody insanity.

They invade your space with uncalled for advice or insults to soften you up but doing the opposite.

It was a system, you were weak then: to recall events anchors you back down and it's grim.

VIOLENCE STAYS IN THE SOUL

It's their violence that stays in the soul. Sudden flare ups by someone who seemed so normal.

A battle of realities and they're crazy but have the upper hand: now you're entering evil territory.

Passing: If last resort grapes don't work then just give them comfort and solace with liquor.

Get the gist/headline then get off the news. Too much redundancy and you've got more to do.

It's so insulting their censorship as if they know true reality and you don't when they're fullabull.

You start a project and someone's at the door. It's too casual a life for those wanting to discover.

A toxic mindset is broken and constantly works against you. Others sense the error and eschew.

PULLING DOWN STRONGHOLDS

Pulling down strongholds: it's a thought system in your head that works against God and yourself.

You're either full throttle ahead or pulled back into your past/fears instead, stuck as the walking dead.

THE BLOODY NERVE

When you're stuck you're vulnerable to the schmuck and it all goes down from there, yuk.

Pulling down strongholds: it's a thought system in your head that works against God and self. **

The right is reacting to leftist fascism and the left will not never believe they are the reason.

A mind is toxic when consciousness is broken, working against your best interests too man.

A SICK SYSTEM USES OUTSIDERS

A sick system incorporates outsiders to target the scapegoat: lawyers, cops, anyone you know.

News: first disaster then hearing crisis stories for months. Never before has man had such stress.

"Whatever they want I fully support". How do you know without knowing what it is, falling short?

Whatever they have to say fits a succinct email, not going on and on in an undisciplined trail.

They always wanna talk on the phone. How I hate it as they bloviate/get on a tangent of long ago.

HEADACHES AND CONFLICT

Unbelievable shame & embarrassment looking back but I had to go thru it to be so staunchly against it.

The headaches don't abate til you solve the conflict inside of going against the Lord's edicts.

My headaches went away when I dropped the contact and punished thoughts of him constantly.

Let walking away gently be amongst your greatest achievements and don't take it lightly.

LOOKING BACK

The Lord our God said to us in Horeb, "You have stayed long enough at this mountain." Deut 1: 6

Yet the righteous holds to his way. He with clean hands grows stronger and stronger. Job 17: 19

No one who puts his hand to the plow and looks back is fit for the kingdom of God. Luke 9: 62

He who began a good work in you will bring it to completion one the appointed day. Phil 1:6

Commit your work to the Lord, and your plans will surely be established. Proverbs 16:3

The saints feel extreme shame and embarrassment but the others couldn't care less: fact.

Pull back from this thing then grieve the disappointment. Forget the person, it's lost hope.

A relative telling you to stay in something like that with an abuser is your enemy not good ol' chap.

Your best friend saying you're right when you're really wrong was a demon enemy all along.

SECRET COALITIONS IN SYSTEMS

Open rebuke is better than secret love, faithful are the wounds of a friend that'll make you good.

Avoid friends who tell you you're good when you're really bad. It's the kiss of an enemy, sad.

Once free the toxic mind talks you back into the bondage: each time love is more like a mirage.

If he hurt you he's toxic no matter how great his reputation, profession or financial situation.

Pay attention to thoughts you always ignored. Debate your own mind, question the siren lures.

Once crossing that line callousness sets in: you become dense to the severity of the sin.

BROKEN QUEEN CONSCIOUSNESS

Broken toxic consciousness: I don't deserve better, I gotta stay in this, I'll tolerate this mess.

Terror at the betrayal from someone you trusted. You rely more on God & less on man, disgusted.

Faced with sudden betrayal I exploded all the time. I had no skill sets to handle social crimes.

All a man wants is tranquility in home but when wife is a drama queen outa nowhere he's done.

You've had enough trauma & loveless relationships. Be EXTRA nice to your spouse for success.

A home should mean comfort and protection from ridicule. Be extra nice to all in your crew.

Soul ties develop around sexual attractions. You should be chaperoned, it's something to fear man.

If you're magnetically/chemically attracted then that's something to question/I'd doubt that.

Don't look for a super hero to pull down those strongholds--you gotta finally mature girl.

A stronghold is a thought system locking bondage in. It is anti-God and anti-YOU so watch it friend.

Fast on outer then go inward---the inner journey is an adventure of enlightenment/you'll soar.

A clear mind makes the right decision despite pain, tears and that magnetic animal attraction.

If your mind is not with common sense you gotta have a conversation with yourself: is it toxic?

TOXICITY TURNS BACK

A toxic mind is so mean to your self it will explode in faux pas in front of superiors, it's hell.

They put all guilts & shames on one, the chosen scapegoat then told him get outa town/GO!

Don't worry, your ship will come in. Maybe not as soon as you thought when young and dumb.

Cast your care on Him. Boxes, shipping containers on Him, keep on piling til misery is gone.

Are you a famous writer or blocked by addiction fitting nowhere with your mind in the gutter?

She's not "waiting for her husband to die". He IS dying and she's just adjusting for survival, aye.

When you turn it all off and get into your own situation you get intuition and miracles happen.

I don't need a mean man, I've had enough of mean men--there's a strain of women-hate in them.

When does news watching become misery porn? Be like the old days just into your own home

THE BLOODY NERVE

They hated Me, they will hate you. They persecuted Me, they will you. Jesus, to His few.

If you adjust to your culture not God you'll be thinking all those wrong and dirty things in the mud.

When a woman chases men who don't want her or resists she puts her mental health at risk.

Unlike the culture around you always bringing you down to immaturity like them, you conform to God.

THE ELITE MYSTICS

In old age the elite are infantile, otherworldly, mystical and definitely the most creative [style!]

You could never have an elite friend acting like you're in high school always with a crowd around.

Infantile: not out there in active mode anymore, it's about relaxing into the inner to explore.

You've completed your work on earth as king now return to the child again, a page eldering.

When you've had enough humiliation and finally stand up for yourself you create, then elation.

Flashbacks/intrusive memories: can happen at any time, destroying day/obstructing mind.

He pays the bills, gives me total privacy and keeps me in good herb, what else is necessary?

Don't be afraid of your new role tho' in some it may bring panic. Change does this, just love it.

It's the rabble who face heart attacks from fear in the latter days. Talk yourself down/be amazed.

No more jet pills/even halves. Those are dangerous but now you're thin energy will be a natch.

PUSH EM TO THE EDGE

Push em to the edge if you can. Can you, do you have the boldness & guts or stay boring Sue?

After 60 the flu can you wipe you out for good or leave you lame. Pine Needles cocktail daily in am.

Your achievement was in not doing more than anything. Sticking to narrow path/nappy with that.

I repent of jet pills. I'm high enough on my own now and besides I've learned/God showed me how.

For me jet bills cause fear of heart attacks which could cause a heart attack so they're dangerous.

My perception was from sin valley but with repentance it all changed back like a new baby.

Success has come for the superior man. After years of thankless trudging he's finally won.

If you look this good you can't be in poor health kid so just enjoy the ride in skinniness for victory.

CHASING WOMEN AND SEX, REJECTION

If a chasing woman uses sex to seal the catch her misery deepens quickly as he surely rejects.

If she does have sex but doesn't make the catch it impacts self-esteem while still attached.

When women lose that chase they believe less and less in their own value: chastity always pays.

THE BLOODY NERVE

He's tough but she's not emotionally equipped to face rejection: don't chase--
that's the reason.

A weak woman who's broken chases, bringing rejection from man which is
most spiritually dangerous.

Women fuse through sex so the postorgasmic withdrawal of the male is a stab
in the back.

You don't just chase/you gotta catch or the rejection quickly sends her
tearfully over the edge.

WOMEN AND REJECTION

Men are built to withstand rejection cuz they're the chasers and women the
choosers/refusers.

Women are not built for serial romantic disapproval so the chase of the females
needs removal.

Let's say she catches him, now she's gotta KEEP him. It's a big/futile job of
pure energy dedication.

But why does she have to "catch" him? Cuz he's running away, giving reason
for the chase.

Once in her grasp how does she keep him there? That's masculine work,
destroying feminine flare.

It's a man's job to figure how to keep a woman, not hers to keep him, the whole
thing's insulting.

The feminine essence is to relax happily into it not to control the man, to do
the "keeping".

She's the one who is kept not the man but it's all reversed and women are
hyper-controllin'

Now you caught him, you gotta keep him. She may even provide for, protect
and preserve him.

A feminine man allows himself to be caught. Now she must cherish him, again taking the man's spot.

CHASING WOMEN ARE NOT VIRTUOUS

To cherish and keep him she must pamper him like he's a woman--keeping him needy is the system.

She's she's playing the man/he's playing the feminine, he may or not have a job or profession.

The chasing woman pays his bills/buys him gifts and other degrading lures to keep his interest.

The man loves his wife as Christ loved [was consumed with] the church, not this crap in reverse.

Catch, keep and cherish is her adopted masculine role. This hasn't a good outcome as she grows old.

The only thing she "catches" is a man who was feminine from the beginning as roles were switched.

A real man wouldn't allow himself to be caught as he avoids her knot so what's she finally got?

The correct way is to become wifely and virtuous so he recognizes you for what you are sis.

The correct way is to become wifely and virtuous, so he recognizes you free of blemish.

DON'T CHASE: BE VIRTUOUS

Most women are either chasing or in the grips of the wrong mate see: rarely is it done rightly.

There is a generation of men who promote chasing as a way to control the soul of broken women.

That type of beta male wants her to pour all her assets out on the ground for him to squander.

The more she invests the more she persists in proving her way's the best and what a mess.

Giving him more property to keep him brings her down into a pit of humiliation until he's gone.

I pray for your disentanglement from a yoke of bondage based on role reversals and their damage.

Why did aunts of old inculcate this concept? Because as birds and the bees it is the most basic.

FINISH ASSIGNMENT, BREAK IN CLOUDS

Finally, a break in the clouds. A refreshing breeze after you have worked and waited so long.

I have finished my assignment: it's locked into place but there's always editing 'til the last minute.

She knows but unlike you doesn't pick fights over the past constantly, just when there's tranquility.

It's no longer a question of how to get to success but how to handle it when you get there sis.

I'm putting boxes and shipping containers on Jesus. He said cast it all on Him to be care-less.

Cast your care or be joyless. It's just too much to be concerned with, must not micromanage it.

She's not a "[put label here]" but a discoverer who had a few incidents in her teens fifty years earlier.

She worked day and night on it for fifty years and finally at 73 she's a success, a multimillionaire.

When falling back into sin you're in a different dominion altogether and it's dangerous let alone no fun.

Grossly exaggerating crimes on the right & never condemning those on the left, they're alright.

Because prophets tell us things we don't wanna hear they're stoned/killed and it's all from fear.

We're being persecuted not just for free speech but wrongthink, falsely accused by sick freaks.

They want us to be careful, to hesitate and to comply. It's a speedbump w/out free speech, aye.

DEMS LIKE DRUNKEN SAILORS

The incompetent who rule us are those who substitute left wing fantasy for real world policy.

Biden doesn't spend like a drunken sailor cuz at least a drunken sailor spends his own money.

If something's wrong with America why are they all coming here? Wise up/appreciate superior.

Italy voted: God, family and country not climate, equity and teaching sex techniques to kiddies.

How is the right "attacking democracy" when 80% want closed borders but they're open anyway?

Murders occurred rarely and everyone talked about it. Now it's every day and we're dead to it.

Greatest were known in the womb before they were born: Jacob, Esau, Samson, Isaiah: NO on abort.

God created & knew who was in the womb. Is this why women post abortion go into depression?

Babies: precious human lives we're supposed to protect but mere unwanted debris to the left.

It's "MAGA extremism" to lower inflation and energy costs, secure the border or jail criminals.

It's not only the Hitlers but **WEAK** leaders that mess things up every time. Biden comes to mind.

WEAK LEADERS OR HITLER

People fear a Hitler but not a weak leader who will always eventually cause total disaster.

Weak leaders: easily bought/taken in by whoever inflates him: subject to changes like the wind.

If it were Trump and his kids the media would have a feeding frenzy but with Biden it's crickets.

"Equity" is just a new age talking point, putting you in a box and creating enemies to target.

"Equity" is just another word for discrimination. These people always label things in opposition.

"Equity" is making up for the past. Hurricane victims should be prioritized by race says VP Harris.

"Equality" is judging by our merit, "equity" is quite the opposite and extremely immoral, RACIST.

Equality is achievement thru equal opportunity, equity is racist policies for equal outcomes.

This new racism of deciding by skin color by VP Harris is purposeful, immoral and calculated.

If only they could look for answers not regress thru immoral politics, not seeing it as inferior.

Crime's on the ballot, no doubt about it. And regarding the border most of us want it closed shut.

AS THE LYMPH CLEANS OUT

As the lymph cleans out you'll see a million bumps--pustules from landmines dispersing up.

As the debris field dislodges from the cell wall it goes thru the blood then erupts thru your bod.

The skin has gotta get worse to get better. Everything's re-assembling as you detox the inferior.

Every time you're zapped it's a new chemical injury which increases your allergic sensitivities.

I gave him Jagermeister, a German tonic for when sick or dying and the bible's concurring.

It has alcohol in it, so what. When dying just make yourself comfy and enjoy a wet lunch.

With fasting, everything has to get worse to get better cuz the crud goes thru the blood til done sir.

Cancer: If grapes don't work then just provide endlife comfort and solace with Jagermeister liquors.

Ageless skin [wrinkles]: Fasting [autophagy] eliminates clogging, triggering collagen production

Collagen production sites clogged with toxins so fast to clean em then ageless skin is comin'.

God did not consign us to ugliness with aging. It's all from toxins building up/a collapsed building.

Altho' collagen production naturally decreases it is still there if it can get thru the crap we wear.

Ladies will get plastic surgery but are any strong enough merely to fast by eating every other day?

Like a clogged pipe it's the rusty sites of collagen production that prevent young skin.

NUTRITION'S AN EXCUSE TO EAT

"Good nutrition" is an excuse to eat. We're talking full throttle ahead for the discoverers/elites.

Einstein proved less is more. That most creative energy comes in least mass and thus I weigh 94.

In Early California men were giants and women Lilliputian but these tiny queens ruled the men.

Pulchritude is not flesh but debris: retained feces and water, up to 25 pounds of it see.

God said to fast/gave me the flue where I couldn't eat anyway and that's just like Him, Dad.

Don't see a doctor they'll prescribe or label it "bipolar". There are two brains, we all have flip flops.

Swear off dangerous jet pills/even halves and now you have God's energy and it's a natch.

Get MANA in there, a gulp from frig: smoothie with 4 bananas/4 peaches/tab almond butter.

Jesus saved me from a heart attack from those damned jet pills, now I have ecstacy and thrills.

There are some things totally legal and totally dangerous, esp for the supersensitives.

The body is like a water-well: the stuff circulates thru each cell and you don't wanna know it all.

GREAT NEWS FOR THE SMART

It's great news for the smart: the system self-corrects so you don't have to work on parts.

Extreme ectomorphy may terrify at first as perception changes but it'll be great so persevere.

I stopped at 94. Nut butters and spuds added or a little cheese on tacos on occasion if I desire.

Having the EE Body means a different perceptual style: a proprioceptive sensory journey--WOW.

Those jet pills miscombined with good herb and i suddenly panicked and ended up in ER.

See yourself as a famous jockey who's gotta be EE to keep his job and be the best at it see?

If it's just me, a little good herb, gulps from the fridge, exercising or just musing it's all ok.

The flue is not just chills & pains it'll leave you flat, dead or lame. Pine Needles daily ma'am.

Had to go offa jet pills because I'm too high on my own. I'm getting hep adapted to a new role.

WAIT FOR THE PEARL

I write it cuz God told me to write it, that's all I know. It's tempered with science in daily memos.

You have nothing to worry about hon' cuz everyone has their day in the sun and you have won.

It's when you take the day off that creative action takes off. Funny it works like that--a little trick.

THE BLOODY NERVE

How can you write if you don't know what to write about? You gotta experience life that's all.

Don't think back to when you had no boundaries and were driven crazy: it's all a system see.

You judge my work because you have a huge fan base and nobody likes me? It's all social see.

Music all day and psych rap, what else you got? It's the story of my life plus the view and walks.

As I look out to eternity I say: thank you God for his day, 365 x a year and many more years I pray.

HOW TO WAIT

HAPPY LIFE FREE OF STRIFE

A whole new vista arises after escaping the painful pugnacious matrix with relational lunatics.

Like a tennis ball held down in water you will shoot up like a miracle after resolving this matter.

The main challenges to God's people are twofold: prayers for HEALING and the problems of WAITING.

I've done my work, God is my Promoter. He designed it, moved me to do it and has the link for it.

How to make the link appear: get rid of everyone else then everything falls together of course.

Time to say goodbye to everything you're known. The Great Division says: Your Time Has Come.

Crossing the Great Divide is this division: If they're not with you 100% then good riddance to em.

This is your last day down with the masses. Now your life will be spectacularly above it all, the joyless.

HOW TO WAIT: DISENTRENCH FROM THE DIS

So count yourself rare and the best, you passed the test to disentrench from all systems who dis.

Narcissism is a growing personality force seen everywhere so all systems have one or more.

Narcissist opinion leader had all the power with her flying monkeys behind her and I was a loner.

HOW TO WAIT

The only way to adapt to a narcissist is with lost reality, low self-worth and feeling you don't exist.

It's a SYSTEM and every leader needs an army. Those are flying monkeys doing dirty work see.

They may be so horrified by what they do remember that all they do is run, hide, push it down.

The past haunts em. No one can outrun trauma and abuse, it always shows itself [e.g. short fuse].

Nightmares, triggers, flashbacks: trauma always raises it's ugly head or in chronic pains instead.

They can't heal cuz they refuse to feel: in dealing with trauma they deny it has any effect at all.

EXTREME VACILLATIONS

Extreme vacillations in appearance indicate a demon or addiction. Sin changes aura colors hon'

It's wrong that your dad beat you daily and girls, it's wrong she bashed you in public honey.

Loving at first, he was an ogre looking thirty years older, out to get me and inciting riots against me.

A dashing handsome gentleman then a ruthless alcoholic and my worst enemy on earth man.

Face it, you were a self-righteous slob and a hick. A dam pagan too marking yourself up like that.

WE WANT NO SOUL TIES

A soul tie is a luring spirit--alluring--but with knowledge you can learn to hate it/resume growing.

HOW TO WAIT

You want no soul ties. They possess your soul [they're all you think about] and block all you know.

If he's all you think about and it's about the bed, that's a soul tie. Become whole and joyous, aye.

Imagine: you have a soul tie to a dirty old man or nasty girl. That's a bad association for sure.

It's like they become part of you--a dirty, inferior, dust on a mirror spiritual tumor and a horror.

Samson the most powerful man on earth was turned into a weasley curse by the Delilah Spirit.

He would rather you suffer than to admit he's wrong on the climate issue, that's the bad leader.

Any goat, cow, horse, cat or dog can have sex. That doesn't show you're superior it's just a fact.

MALIGNANT NARCISSISM

A malignant narcissist is easily offended. They go to war with the slightest slight so get fenced.

The revenge sought is very disproportionate to the narcissistic injury in the first place, believe it.

Since malignants don't have a conscience they do things normal people would never consider sis.

They have zero accountability and in fact their victims get used to taking the blame already.

He is very impulsive with extremely low impulse control. A true reactor whom I wouldn't trust at all.

They are sadistic and take pleasure as others suffer. Esp if you hurt em in some way, beware.

HOW TO WAIT

The sadistic tormenting of others/family is a very large part of narcissistic supply.

A highly empathic member of the system has cognitive dissonance, unable to understand a sadist.

They feel pathological envy with every fiber of being, doing terrible things to alleviate jealousy.

It was a Pyrrhic Victory: she won the battle but lost the war, what she came here for--to go far.

She won the battle [making me apologize & kowtow] but I never wanna see her again the mad cow.

WHEN I THINK OF YOU

Let go of/transcend constraints on consciousness. That means him or her, this is the elder gist.

When I think of you I'm sad. I'm gonna seclude to the pad, forget you ever existed and be glad.

When I think of you I feel anxious competitive strivings of the herd mind so I'm staying home, aye.

When I think of you I feel competition with your whole stable and to queens this is unacceptable.

An elder doesn't put up with things. Grow up--lay down lines and make em stick, be rightly/kingly.

PROJECTION OF JEALOUSY

Narcissists start out by believing others are jealous and that brings them great joy and happiness.

With time this becomes paranoia, as their sins are magnified in the supposed focus on em.

HOW TO WAIT

They project what they think and feel onto others. He's out to get them = they're out to get HIM.

When malignant narcissists are challenged/exposed or threatened there is explosive dangerous rage.

Even ONE exposure to the rage of a malignant narcissist make become complex trauma for life sis.

MN rage is a permanent personality/character disorder and there's only one solution: escape now.

You committed the most blasphemous evil of simply pointing him out and it was blast off.

His malignant rage reset my clock for life. My whole world view changed in one minute, aye.

You push the envelope and you lose some but not others. Those are forgivers: the keepers.

SMALL TOWN SMOTHERING

They escaped small towns where their life was an open book and started new lives private for good.

Gossip. In a small town you never stamp it out and just to see your reaction they'll bring it up.

From life as an open book to living the high life behind a big wall and locked gate is paradise ok.

In a small town you meet your enemies at the post office. Enough of that crap, alone at last.

In a small town the false accusations gain speed and they've all agreed you're the worst fiend.

I relocated to a country neighborhood where no one even cares they're so inner-directed to home.

HOW TO WAIT

ETERNAL: TRANSCENDING PEOPLE

One generation is warped, the next one far more warped and the next one is lost and beyond hope.

People lose significance when realizing you leave the earth alone. Focus on words from above.

When you die Jesus is there to usher you into eternity not your neighbors, family or frenemies.

Always worrying what they saying or doing and if they're attending or disapproving. This is insanity.

Especially when you see their rejection is used as a rudder for control so we stay in safe zones.

To Y'All: These social devices to control consume half our lives or more and I'm through with it all.

UNRESOLVED TRAUMAS TO THE CORE

The unresolved trauma drills down to the core and they end up with physical diseases like cancer.

As they rot they still can't admit the truth that YES they rejected the best in serving the narcissist.

As they've covered everything the narcissist has done, they themselves end in pain/bedlam.

Monkeys are characterized by sudden amnesia: "I never said that, you're imagining things" etcetera.

They'll always shift the blame to you, the oversensitive drama queen who's probably insane too.

If you're the only one confronting narcissistic abuse you'll be the only one on a healing path too.

HOW TO WAIT

They never defend you or stand up for you cuz they lack the guts to walk away from the narcissist.

They have no grit, they have no guts to reject the narcissist as you did, the escape artist.

It's just too easy for the weak to stay in the "we" crowd not go with you, the ostracized called odd.

The monkeys putting you down don't have the guts you do so you win, hoo hoo, for being strong.

Monkeys will bully, gaslight and manipulate as they lie, steal, and conceal legal information ok.

Have you not noticed how annoying sidekicks refuse to see the truth of their nefarious leader?

WEAK LEADERS HAVE ARMIES

It's a SYSTEM and every leader needs an army. Those are flying monkeys doing dirty work see.

The worst army leaders are women: Jezebels who in weakness must galvanize their angry men.

I was shocked at how horribly her friends treated me. I never knew them, they were primed by she.

Dirty work, dirty work: that's all you've had due to this system of bad leaders under a dam curse.

Due to weakness the narcissist must have cohorts who are so weak they can't get away like us.

It takes a strong and courageous person to leave all you know behind but a better life arrives.

To them everything is your fault cuz "it's all of us against YOU" but that's the mobbing mentality too.

HOW TO WAIT

They are naive cowards who are complicit to abuse. They love doing the work for the narcissist.

Working for the narc is the path of least resistance to fools, teacher's pets, bureaucrats, rats.

And once they're in the loop they just shut it all down totally to the scapegoat, odd man, fool.

ECCENTRICS LIVE TEN YEARS LONGER

Eccentrics--loners--live an average of ten years longer. From what I've described is it any wonder?

The minute you're outa the system you're just a name or story. You're free that's all, no more worries.

What's the natural human mentality as one approaches death? More monk-like, separate.

They will gaslight, provoke and mob you with smear campaigns cuz you escaped the system.

How dare you illuminate a situation which is so psychologically abusive, you're oversensitive.

So now you know who's superior to who. You escaped and they didn't, the enmeshed victim tools.

You may have been mobbed yet felt all just agreed with the narcissist, not that he asked for assist.

They punish the scapegoat for setting boundaries and will double up if they go no-contact [free].

SINISTER PEOPLE LIE, CHEAT, STEAL

They are gonna lie, cheat and steal as sinister people do: seek out and hurt the truthseeker too.

HOW TO WAIT

The scapegoat IS the empath, the stronger more courageous person and thus they hate him.

They're so jealous they must do something, and typically it's illegal, criminal and sinister.

They didn't TELL him the details of the estate for his own inheritance, they meddled in the mess.

They didn't TELL him that he got half the house or that if he dies it all goes to THEIR relatives.

Will signing and inheritance time flushes out all these sinister hypocritical horrible human foibles.

MONKEYS ARE TWO FACED

The monkeys have Jekyll and Hyde double personalities. Syrupy sweet with scriptures hiding daggers.

"Oh, if you only saw her true colors you may think otherwise about her..." and innuendos so clever.

Half truths, outright slander and vicious lies. Jezebel does it best in balancing all you guys.

All because she's jealous of how you look or act, or how impervious you are to her--there's always that.

They live double lives. Their public personna is good hearted people while being evil as hell.

All that matters is you saw through the smokescreen and you do know the truth, now renew.

They criticize your failings/never stop cuz deep down they're cowards, not confident enough to favor.

The only way these weaklings can feel good is to puff themselves up while tearing you down.

HOW TO WAIT

You must be radically relieved to see it hasn't been your imagination, it was all a god-hating system.

Studying monkeys and narcissists we see it had nothing to do with us, it was them and the system.

TOXIC, SINISTER, DEMONIC PEOPLE

Toxic, sinister, demonic people are global because the bible said it's a **WIDE** path to hell.

It made them feel better about themselves to tear you down, which they did constantly to anyone around.

The only way to feel good about themselves. Who does that? A coward who's miserable, no success.

By going no contact they've lost control of you so will now control how others see you.

All of the monkeys triangulate so you soon see to reject all connections secondary and tertiary.

Being more affluent they could hire lawyers against me. They were part of the system of treachery.

Lawyers were fed all the family mythology and untruths against me and joined in the spree.

SECONDARY MONKEYS: LAWYERS

This scapegoat role is extremely common but you may feel isolated, misunderstood and mobbed.

Shyster believes sister about the scapegoat without judge nor jury and now he's part of the club.

Who's paying? The narcissist so the attorney's all for her and will assist in slaying the dissident.

HOW TO WAIT

They will do anything to trash your public reputation with family, friends, neighbors, coworkers.

It will come out in the wash, be still. Nothing's hidden from God and making it even is His will.

They will triangulate your relationship to strangers. What they want is to annihilate you forever.

They want to destroy YOU cuz you are a reminder of what they're not and they don't know God.

They're not strong, empowered empaths who are transparent and brave, they only hate.

After escaping the vicious/malicious attacks of the narc and monkeys we rise to the top in Victory.

I'm sorry you had to go thru this, I'm sorry I had to too. But what's come from it is gold/new crew.

You've done the work and God is the Rewarder cuz He's not a jerk like those who used you, stole, usurped.

GOD'S TIMING

Success is in the air, the seasons have changed, everything's opening up-- seems so strange.

I was hidden under God's hand for years, decades. To be exposed in open seems incredibly strange.

Solution: Just keep doing what you're doing. Whatever's in front, concentrate on that darling.

"My time has not come" Jesus said to His disciples as they bugged him constantly to do His thing now.

When my time has come I'll not be able to not do it. Please know that, it's patience not cowardice.

HOW TO WAIT

There is a time for all things. Until the time comes to arise, it's still time to stay humbly low, then the prize.

God will bring you forth in HIS timing and any rushing before completion only brings humiliation.

Be an ageless child not a neurotic adult. Like an unplanned day of play, fall into what God's prepared you nut.

God will just bring you out and suddenly the spotlight's on you. No one to see, nothing to do, just cruise.

LIFE IS BRAND NEW EACH MORNING

Let life be brand new every morning. Clear the slate & start over remembering God is the Almighty.

You've planted the seed now how to wait: Realize you must get outa God's way because it's planned fate.

How to wait: Get outa God's way man. He can't do all He needs to do blocked by your petty plans.

You wait by looking out the window. By stopping frenetic work and becoming one with elements, all aglow.

Living in a small liberal desert town was hell. The things that happened I hate thinking about or to tell.

I'm not a dam liberal nor a prosperity teacher either--although I think it can be done cuz God is so clever.

If He put that bee in your bonnet He also picked the link. Stay free of the stink and wait for golden ring.

Instead of persistent anger at your unwanted guests ask yourself what YOU did to attract these pests?

God has ONE right link all planned and no one else can do it on the planet so just clear the way darnit.

HOW TO WAIT

Hang on to God your only Promoter. He is your champion cuz you're His kid and He your Provider.

GOD GAVE YOU IDEAS AND HE HAS THE LINK

He would have never given you these ideas if He didn't have the link to their success--that's who He is.

Stop scrambling for idiots who can't help you. They're bores/conformists who are going nowhere too.

Let go of evil helpers--make a space. This is pneumaticity: you won't attract the LINK until they're erased.

After going through that mediocre condescension I'm happy to work alone until My Time Has Come.

Your work is done only to face the next obstacle: staying cheerful while waiting and refusing to buckle.

Success doesn't happen right away: few experience this, ok? You must learn to wait for your payday.

You've done the Great Work--God approves. Now you wait to show yourself faithful THEN He moves.

Don't get dis-couraged while you wait. That's right: courage is just waiting without losing faith.

I will wait as long as you say Father. I know My Day is Coming because your are faithful to me your daughter.

It's not about shaking hands in Boca Raton but doing your work even if its in a lonely ghost town.

REST after ripoff and before rule: Sleep and relax as much as you can cuz you were DRAINED by fools.

SOLITUDE LOVERS ARE "HATERS"

They'll call you a "hater" for staying freer. If you want solitude they'll take it as an insult if you won't cater.

HOW TO WAIT

I've done enough damage today--think I'll rest and relax to get ready for tomorrow, a new day.

You surrounded yourself with users constantly taking things from you--that's not freedom it's staying blue.

Just continue your work in your own personal monastery until your time comes--and it certainly will, hon'.

So you wasted your time and money with these losers. Just pay them off and go on as space cruisers.

If they have no lines you'll be constantly surprised. Get walled in then feel disgust for the hypnotized.

MUST SOAR LIKE THE EAGLES

You can't soar with the eagles by flying with the turkeys they say--so good riddance to them today.

Even letting em in without calling is a terrible compromise, when you wanted to do what you like.

You must constantly prune, simplify and streamline your life--that includes bad vibrations creating strife.

All I can say is Thank you Father for making me the author of a great and marvelous work and wonder!

One touch of favor is worth more than a lifetime of labor.

For Daniel, trouble was a setup to bring him into prominence. See DOWNS as opportunity and promise!

See this era of "nothing happening" as a sign something's about to explode all over the map hon'.

Favor won't keep you out of the lion's den but will keep the lions from harming you as God's children.

Challenges come to us all but God's favor is why you don't STAY down. Trust in that and look UP to God.

HOW TO WAIT

NOTHING'S HAPPENING SO YOU'LL RELY ON GOD

Nothing's happening: more reason to totally lean on God. We've become weak: that's what He wanted.

I felt like I waited forever but with faith it finally exploded all over and now all I say is God is so clever!

Hope deferred makes the heart sick but a longing fulfilled is a tree of life: This is the cycle of hope/strife.

Joseph visited the pharaoh as a prisoner and walked out later as the prime minister: that's favor.

The issue with favor is it happens SUDDENLY. Just knowing this gives us hope it can happen TODAY.

God will favor me for talking about God's favor for free so I will wait until the day when God showers me.

After years of unremunerated work and frustration in one hour you're catapulted to the highest station.

When God just breathes on you supernatural doors will open/obstacles looking permanent turn around.

The greater opposition the more God's endorsement, the more enemy attacks the better we are for em.

Like a bow and arrow: The enemy thinks he's pulling you back but only makes you shoot further, wow!

Favor looking up: When God says it's time you shoot into new levels of leadership/prominence.

Right now God works behind the scenes setting you up for His endorsement so sit tight and wait for Him.

DESTINY MOMENTS ARE LINED UP

God has destiny-moments already lined up for you--you can't see it now but suddenly you're brand new.

HOW TO WAIT

I was troubled for 23 years but it only took an hour to be resolved--that's how God works: the Great Salve.

God said "Joshua, today is your moment, I'm gonna show the people the greatness I put in you" amen?

God knows how to endorse you and make your life significant--it's not meaningless if diligent.

All creation is waiting for the day when the children of God are revealed for how great they are: stars!

Keep honoring God and He'll show the world how great you are with great prominence as stars.

God's children are not just stars but meant to accomplish things of great significance in a fallen world.

Stop cheerleading other people! God wants YOU to shine and accomplish great things/the impossible!

Creativity, ability, courage and strength is flowing through you now just by knowing your Father, God.

Do miracles, accomplish the impossible, achieve art and science discoveries--the new notables!

Just look at the crap that is lauded in society. It's nothing, boring, dirty, godless, and without any variety.

God's favor causes you to stand out and be preferred--no matter who competes with you, they're slurred.

Success comes not from east or west but God who puts you up and the other down as second best.

WE'VE BECOME CULTURALLY INSANE

We've become culturally insane since then and it's reflected in fashion: Paris runways show bedlam.

HOW TO WAIT

What ages and kills faster than disease? SIN. Don't forget that man, you're lookin' pasty/haggard again.

It's just the way it's gotta be: I hardly ever see him but he's protecting me. THIS is the life for The Lady.

His most important job is to keep people away. Never forget the worst thing is a porous boundary.

Take on a god archetype then the minute you slip up it's the Fallen Hero Syndrome--watch out my son.

Fortunately, there'll only remain your perfect works and nothing about when you were a sinner/jerk.

She doesn't wanna compete with all those other women. She's superior to your crowd/must stay dim.

THEY STATE THE OBVIOUS

He does a marvelous job of stating the obvious but does he have a point or does he rant on the irrelevant?

Marriage is coming within walls. That's what I want: total protection and the daily reality of a household.

Feminists see marriage as captivity and for false narratives and liberal ideals they'll bitch to eternity.

Picture our home as a castle surrounded by a molt with armed guards and dogs--this is of God!

Once clear of people and past we penuriously choose back who we want, with much thought.

This is my reality and to a social man I would seem anti-society but it's really about self and family.

It's about making sure our lives continued AS-IS with six months food supply, things like that/no lack.

HOW TO WAIT

Because it's all about HOME, HOME, HOME. Men go to war to defend home and the country it's in.

There was a time I didn't see a need for a fence and locked gate. In this era I was neurotic, crazy and irate.

What has made you so pathetic suddenly? Why have the archetypes flipped seemingly beyond remedy?

What has made you age overnight? What did you do to change your physiognomy looking like a fright?

If you're still not right something will happen in front of the whole world now: when exposed don't go low!

It is a horrible thing to witness one's depedestalization especially publicly but yes, it happened to me.

MUST BUILD BACK UP

It was followed by decades in solitude building back up, on the potter's wheel and enjoying the silence.

I lost everything and had just the basics. I learned the essentials of home as protection from lunatics.

Home creation and maintenance is a full time job if it is to inspire those who live there with female flair.

Is your home female-influenced or feminist-influenced? For there's a black and white difference you dunce.

Silence is the best response to a fool. Don't fight for identity--stay quiet/work towards the goal.

A splendid home is an otherworldly atmosphere of little charming nooks/unique things to look at.

A splendid home is picked up ready for a new day. Don't leave things lying around/get some class ok?

HOW TO WAIT

If a "friend" brings his friends and you're offended by them then ditch him too due to bad associations.

If you can't stand against ridicule you simply isolate yourself. With age it's even more pronounced.

All you gotta do is be my fence and take care of business and I'll do the rest with my presence.

We'll make money with the colab--perhaps it's what destiny's waiting for, alone we stay trapped.

For alone I'm great but in a crowd I'm so angry or jittery I can't wait to get back to my monastery.

I can't stand ridicule cuz the feminists attacked and I ended in a hospital. They are vicious, I was vulnerable.

The constant nitpicking, accusations, railroading, one-upping, gossiping, spying: they love hating.

SEPARATE PROTECTED SOLITUDE

I think we could be happy together if you'd just leave me alone/I'll leave you alone as we build our home.

I doubt you'll find a woman like this, most are social and will miss their friends--the ones you dismiss.

It's just me. I'm not social, I work day and night in my little room and I'd leave you alone in your solitude.

But I'd be there if you need me, how could you get a better deal than that, that's total protection/liberty.

But then there's the nights. Well that's another thing but it's true you have to eventually stop work/relax.

I get a spot of sun for Vitamin D while enjoying all that I see then I come back in, recharged and ready.

HOW TO WAIT

When she came into my life it was constant trouble and when she went out I was ecstatic/stable.

Why do you call it a lame excuse? Do you even know how conservative women/writers are abused?

No matter how big he thinks he is or gets, sin makes him ugly and brings him down again and again.

It reminds me of Lonesome Roads, a Face in the Crowd: his ego takes off and he's just a loudmouth.

I see him twice a day for home business then get back to writing for the masses. Solitude, almost always.

Get outa yourself and be owned by the world. Repent of memory quicksand/get clarity/go forward girl.

FLYING MONKEY HATRED [BAD ASSOCATIONS]

When they met me all they knew was hatred and wanting to destroy me. These were women, see?

Many women are creepy witches and they don't even know why they're jealous. They just hate ya bitch.

All they knew when they met you was they were gonna get you and SOON. This is the jungle of women.

Women are witches who work in networks and it's the worst kind of tyranny and social curse.

Mimicking mom could get you killed. Be aware of your environment, not everyone is so unstable.

He's not an intellectual if playing silly games online and drinking. Intellect is not about memorizing.

It's the women who get men fired, who proclaim "I'm gonna get him" as all their friends chime in.

HOW TO WAIT

I don't like Cults of Self they give me the creeps/seem weird and I'd rather stick to science dear.

If a Cult of Self becomes a Lonesome Roads the whole paper palace implodes--that's fame ya' know.

You've endured the job of reviewing your history with new eyes, now return to the beginning/be wise.

THINK BACK to the most exciting/optimistic fruitful time of your life. Keep that consciousness/stay high.

I swam in muddy waters: went crazy mal-adapting to an abnormal culture and now praise God it's over.

I don't like the Santa Claus thing I prefer the goatee but it's none of my business, it's up to thee.

HARD LESSONS: NEVER AGAIN

It took years of hard lessons realizing it was people making me sick in adaptation, if alone I was an angel.

Your circumstances are good but your mind is tripping you up, making a big deal out of nothing or dust.

Does it make sense that nothing bad's happening but you're feeling crazy? That's dysfunction, amazing.

I dream of that day when everything breaks open and
years of work finally brings remuneration.

When ten becomes 100, then 1000, then a million cuz that's how the internet works--geometric expansion.

How mal-adaptive: Nothing bad's happening at all yet you're crazy with frenetic imaginations.

A change of seasons has occurred--I'm coming out, success is near after obscurity for years.

HOW TO WAIT

You don't understand. God has it all planned. Man plans, God laughs: certainty of success is essential man.

COUNT ON GOD'S FAVOR

Count on God's favor, not how thinks look--ignore all that as false appearance your Father God forsook.

Tho' many students deserved the scholarship God picked you--He knows how to give you breakthrough.

They can't put their finger on why you stand out but God made you attractive, original and powerful, wow!

Favor is more powerful than your resume or qualifications. All worldly red tape is voided by God's directions.

When God opens doors you'll ask "how did I get here--I was the least likely one" and be astonished, hon'

Esther never dreamed of becoming a queen but on that day God turned her to prominence with great sheen.

God will cause opportunity to come to you. Esther never sought that position but it came to her--so cool!

You've worked hard and when God knows He can trust you He'll bring you from obscurity to notoriety.

The waiter--one who waits--may go back into anger/blaming God rather than just continuing on.

It's almost like it feels good--scratches an itch--to blame/hate God since you gotta blame someone.

You've done your work, planted a seed, now you wait. Energy goes to frustration but don't take the bait.

The devil is very good at drawing people away from the things which are most important to them.

We may think we're waiting on God but to be honest, He's waiting on us.

HOW TO WAIT

WAITING: We may think we're waiting on God but to be honest, He's waiting on us. Joyce Meyers

If I don't get what I want will I still love God as much as when I do get what I want: that's the test/no fun.

He humbled/allowed you to hunger, feeding you with manna so you'd know man doesn't live by bread alone.

Lesson: Your joy can't be connected to people's likes, the size of your ministry or smiles on their faces.

Addicted to complements/encouragement: I was there man. So God removed em so I'd want only Him.

Dependent on gofers to always validate you, make you feel good about yourself: God removes this stuff.

Validation only comes from God so relying on people for it means disappointment/feeling odd

KK THOUGHTS WHILE WAITING

These are all my thoughts while waiting, the most essential part. So I think they may be pithy, an art.

A self-righteous slob: that's what we were running with the mob thinking we knew it all.

These are the thoughts of someone WAITING for the new life--going back, re-experiencing strife.

You've been so focused on work you haven't seen the larger picture. That's what the waiting is for.

Our world is failing, we live on the razor's edge--things about to blow wide open but God gave us a hedge.

When I first started school the kids creeped me out--like a psychic scream, I wanted to go home.

HOW TO WAIT

Morals and order broke down after the war. These were their kids and their homes showed disorder.

They creeped me out then so you can imagine the horror being around their great-grandchildren.

Things like going to the bathroom with the door open--I hated those people! They are gross, phony, unkind.

CREEPED OUT BY MY GENERATION

I was so creeped out with this generation I just watched old movies of previous eras lived by mom and dad.

They were sick with their secret pornography collections. The sick creeps behind their image-magic.

We are told to hate everything God hates. The false notion that God only loves is just the sinful new age.

I had to leave a liberal desert town for it's debaucheries. Like ten cars parked at tiny home just for orgies.

As recently as 80's people were sane, well-dressed, decent tho' sinners. Now, open debauchery/monsters.

The white man freed the slaves and democrats were the slaveowners and the KKK, ok?

The freedom to offend is a fundamental part of freedom of speech, and I don't want to befriend those creeps.

Pathological altruism, progressive myopia and cultural capitulation means Paris is a shithole like the nations.

THE BIG SUCK: Incentives for the masses to come to the United States with great good luck.

DEGENERATION OF BLOODLINES

It's called DYSEUGENICS: the degeneration of bloodlines as each generation is worse than the last.

HOW TO WAIT

One generation makes a ton of money and the next becomes wasteful, evil, debauched, suicidal.

What's it all come down to? Loss of morals as each generation becomes more tolerant of the bawdy: calamity.

When they keep asking you what words mean it means they spent their school years in only sexuality.

When you can get people to accept wanton sex it will possess them totally until walking zombies, hexed.

Wanton incessant sex stops their growth: it's the major way Satan warps the mind of the youth.

Just like happened with the Puritans, society was SO debauched they had to go to the other extreme I guess.

The Puritans found that if they didn't go the other extreme their thoughts were tainted with the obscene.

There's a collective unconscious and if it's all about sex the whole thing stinks so the Puritan defects.

They did this to us knowing demoralization makes us defenseless so the Puritans came against this.

Whenever you feel hated for your conservative views it brings relief to recall how they hated Trump too.

DUMB WOMEN AND TRUMP-HATRED

How could you possibly hate Trump that much--are you insane or trying to get approval from the inane?

She doesn't know what she's talking about but so needy her Trump-hatred to the herd goes to extreme.

Inter-group hatred growing as rapidly as Nazi Germany--it's scary, don't underestimate mob psychology.

HOW TO WAIT

I'm so sick of these people I can't stand it--can't wait to get back to the pad/my own life and revel in it.

Every woman I meet spews out the narrative. I never knew women were this dumb, I'm surprised by it.

They act like the more they hate Trump the more they get approval of the other women--it's embarrassing.

For the greatest loss of freedom--a real prison--is having to adapt to other people/made to like em.

The EVENT is over. Can you take it with you? What's the use? Just stay home and mentally cruise, aloof.

God'll take you up--just to give you a taste. Then He pulls the rug out if you're not in step, out of grace.

It happened to me, it was so frightening! Ontologically fatal insight: I was sunk and life was a tragedy.

If you don't know the attributes/laws of God and follow the liberal narrative you'll be sunk too, a pejorative.

If you think that crap is ok and you encourage others to do the same you'll meet your end and it's soon.

You put down our great president but when further questioned about it you shut up or run away you lizard.

You don't know what you're talking about and it's the women who are the problem: take their vote!

HIX POLITIX

TDS means: Can't get past personal feelings to appreciate what Trump did which was epic.

Left wants a destructive, suicidal, unworkable, technologically unfeasible Green New Deal.

HOW TO WAIT

In America to silence em you cancel em but in Russia/most of the world you simply kill em.

Not about communism but Peter the Great/Stalin: heros bringing Russian lands under one rule.

Everyone has a knife but not all are willing to use it. Putin is willing to use it and is doing it.

If you refuse to talk politics soon inferior men will have rule over you and then how will ya like it.

Putin can only work with puppets not free people who want freedom and not willing to give it up.

Biden's more worried about Putin losing than Ukraine winning and that's insane. Lindsey Graham

SUCCESS MAKES A HUGE MESS

Success is too much for em, the ego takes over, they buy everything in sight whether needed or not.

When unhappy after buying everything and getting worse after drugs and things it's the end, a downswing.

When a man can afford his addictions they become bottomless pits and the end is inevitable, it's the pits.

Who learns penuriousness except she who has been through all this? With temperance life is bliss.

I had to withdraw from the noise and madness entirely. Dallas re-runs from the 70's: return to beginnings.

These people are crazy, everything about it is crazy. Trump rallies are groovy but the rest: remove me.

You're not gonna degrade my precious mind with your bullshit, I'll say it. Trump does/keeps our minds lit.

HOW TO WAIT

Dallas re-runs from the seventies: No trash, no homeless people, no heroine addicts just J.R.'s evils.

The seventies: People dressed nice and they were SKINNY! No one's that thin now due to chemicals, see?

Test: Can you become rich and still be humble, restrained and temperate? (Eye of needle and all that).

It's just between you and God now--forget herd and all you knew entirely! God's important not the laity.

I've learned to write these things and not care what they think. Say it then relax into leisure/stay in the pink.

Saturdays meant the joy of being alone, away from school children and I hated groups since back then.

The past is an anchor to the old life and a mine field (more like a grenade range) keeping you in strife.

Being weak incites crafty opposition. This is what every woman must learn or be overcome by bums.

Being weak at boundary-assertion made me a sitting duck. I let him in to destroy me/not "bad luck".

PEOPLE WORSHIP REPLACES GOD

We're are THEISTS--we gotta worship something. So now we worship people but God is seen as nothing.

These words will not be accepted without total revolution: They precede it, they trigger moral indignation.

It's a moral revolution not a political one although one tends to follow the other all through history son.

What you are doing is absolutely in God's will but it will make you alone yet never lonely or bored still.

False or no success: play to the herd for likes. True success: Talk truth whether they like it or not.

HOW TO WAIT

I could NOT believe it when you dropped Christ for Hindu gods. Poverty torn India had 3 million of em.

Christianity enables capitalism that enriches you, me, all of us but you're a godless communist?

I couldn't BELIEVE when you abandoned Jesus in the seventies to read, read, read about Hindu deities.

Read, read, read yet still no POWER. I guess those new age hippy philosophies were your finest hour.

We're all one? The whole world should get together, are you kidding me? We should be separate and free.

Write write write whether they read or like it or not. Write write write cuz it's just between you and God.

I would never rent again. My first live-in brought a bunch of people over and I immediately got rid of him.

HUGGIN' AND KISSIN' IS SICKENIN'

What makes em think they can bring a buncha people to your home? The 70's humanist social syndrome.

"Dallas" had open doors: you met whoever came in. To me that's insane: the greatest wealth is for vettin'

Without a wall and a locked gate what good is your home? This isn't the fifties when you could trust everyone.

Women are always huggin' and kissin' and it's sickening. Don't you know spirits are transferred Missy?

Upon meeting my mom she started hugging and kissing her patronizingly and mom ousted her quickly.

Get some class: Aristocratic Reserve. Stop hugging and kissing you lessie phonies, the very nerve!

How can men be intimidated by creepy ladies always hugging and kissing each other in their groupies?

HOW TO WAIT

America began by Puritans–Calvinists like myself. They were serious, sober and public affection-less.

Every single woman I met who I found intelligent suddenly turned on me for loving Trump, in a minute.

I'm sorry, I just don't respect their intelligence. Yet these women have made y'all beta males, out to lunch?

The epitome of female insanity called "intelligence" is "The View" of course. Asses, silliness, arrogance.

It's called "found time": how much time you get back not watching any more political videos--just home.

They're all dead now. Who cares, they didn't like me then anyhow.

WORDS CREATED WORLD: WATCH 'EM GIRLS

It's about WORDS. God spoke and created the world.

What a way to subvert and overtake a nation: Get em hooked on wanton sex to their own destruction.

Stop thinking of their horrors just spend every waking moment walling up from them, then you'll have bliss.

Like an old cat you reach a point where you've had it and it shows on your face--greatness in any case.

The kissy huggy ladies are on the prowl again but the Trumpsters they won't have as friends, amen?

Just one good picture, Missy. Don't show your wanton narcissism with your constant incessant selfies.

Never forget the main point: by the mere CONTACT they conquer you. CONTACT = CONQUEST.

I'm just the writer, you will not see me. Whether dead or alive it's all about the COPY.

HOW TO WAIT

I DON'T WANNA GO ANYWHERE

I can't have any part of the wanton generation and nor should you. This gives us "found time" for sure.

I suddenly woke up to what happened then. Those gems, pearls of wisdom in our highest stage of eldering.

If I never have to see anyone again it will be my greatest respite and reason for constant thanksgiving.

It's not that I don't like you, I just want solitude. It's not that I hate people just myself more, sorry dude.

They disgust me and bring horror. They depress me and some are whorish. God help me, come Lord.

That's just one little bit of data in a sea of infinite bits of data so forget it, they won't even think of it.

Crazy feminists who hate white men for toxic masculinity LOVE Jihadists--the alpha males of Islam--huh?

GORGEOUS FLOTUS. Not a demeaning hippopotamus like the last one who imposed on us.

SO YOU SCREWED UP, SO WHAT

Controlling your enemies by getting dirt on em--that's what it's all about. Back and forth, roundabout.

So I screwed up, who hasn't? Just return to the right path and forgive yourself cuz it had a price/is finished.

Biggest price was Christ's death so say "it is finished" and sins are as far away as East from West.

It is finished, I have given birth to the Creative Act. It took four decades in fact and a gift to those held back.

HOW TO WAIT

Through clever and shrewd manipulation with words I shatter mindsets like a machine gun, all of em.

With repentance your reality changes and it's like God erases bad history and you just recall the good.

I do remember the lessons that came from all that crap I endured. Like other people imposing forever.

Accept that you must live in a separate reality to be happy. You're that different so manage it honey.

True love conquers all, crooked path straightens out. Public loves happy endings, forget it all/look up.

They wrote you off--due to age, low wage, whatever. Do your thing then don't talk to em again/sever.

They walked you by like you're not worth a dime. God'll show the world who you are and they're slime.

LOOKING BACK BRINGS PANIC, DON'T DO IT

It's not happening now so don't panic looking back. You've grown since then & wouldn't experience that.

Nothing's happening now, you're in safety. But due to PTSD you're back in the trenches of yesterday.

These bad memories act as little anchors to the past--to that level when you groveled, and it was awful.

Try to deal with it once and for all then don't go back. Put it all in a bag then throw the whole bag out.

Out of all the things he could worry about, Paul's whole thing was forgetting the past and pressing on.

If you keep going back your self-esteem will deflate and your reality go black. It's essential to sack it.

Get off work and just do movies, music or nature. You're too tunnel-visioned, widen your scope sir.

HOW TO WAIT

Life is two-pronged: beginning/end, preparation/success. You're here now, don't think back to less.

Pay more attention to the people in your situation. Get off the computer and that's the vacation.

Your husband, the neighbor who's sick, the old cat you took in, new lists for shopping, just appreciating.

Mental transport: Get outa this dirty era by old movies which are time capsules to a decent time.

God's getting ready to bring you out so get ready and take a nap.

Your ageism is worse than racism cuz it disables us. We never even thought of our age we just work a lot.

I must live in my own creative reality--separately--to be happy. I found that out from invasion, unfortunately.

CONTACT = CONQUEST

The social generation lost sight of the extreme influence of contact = conquest making us accept the pests.

The social generation takes your need for solitude as a personal insult and could even get violent about it.

A skid row bum has no privacy, a prison inmate no privacy nor a silly woman without boundaries.

The more I wanted solitude the more they sought to invade me and they were rude--demanding/officious too.

Marriage brings a whole new set of boundaries to be made--establish this before/call a spade a spade.

Stepchildren, the in-laws: hopefully it all goes smooth for y'all--or how your own acts with them, I recall.

Most have unholy alliances and that's all brought in, I can't lie about it-- entanglements vs. staying lit.

HOW TO WAIT

Retirement or eldering is like slipping into cozy pajamas after nervous constraint to conform in America.

Doing/saying what you want with no fear or reprisal sitting behind fence and locked gate is highest fate.

You don't have to show em. God wants to show em and it'll be a much bigger and impressive program.

If you're into success, don't go back to the frustrations of preparation when you couldn't manage the herd/kin.

GOD WANTS TO BRING YOU OUT!

God WANTS to bring you out, to strut your stuff. Your light not under a bushel and speaking against guff.

There is no bigger torture than not being able to assert boundaries while flooded with scoundrels/robbers.

I hated every minute but was trained to be social. Eventually I got over this and stayed private and mindful.

Introverts, cerebrotonics and eccentrics UNITE! We've just as much right to live this way/free of the fight.

The worst plight is to be an introvert married to a social who lets em all in, even without first announcing.

I could be so happy alone then he'd let em all in and I was suddenly like a cat in a roomful of rocking-chairs.

The marriage broke up over it. Good riddance, punk!

No I don't wanna go anywhere. No I don't want them here. I just wanna be alone even from you dear.

They chum up too easily and even have sex casually. They are "loose" and out of order, unreliable, liars.

HOW TO WAIT

The feelings of being invaded: I still feel like a cat in a room full of rocking chairs--will I ever get over it?

Rule of Silence in monasteries: don't talk! it's all inner, silence, ruminating, resolving, talking to God.

I was mesmerized and fell when back to the original system: same grease made the same wheels turn.

Going back always means re-experiencing strife, a demon sent from hell to destroy your very life.

GOING BACK TO THE PITS

Forget the lessons in the pits.

Used to be every man's your friend 'til they show you otherwise, now no one's your friend/they're all disguised.

Trouble was a setup to endorse Daniel and bring him into prominence. That's how God works: paradox.

He spoke worlds into existence, flung stars into space. Don't you think He can bring you out/sins erased?

Strife will block your success, so of course God's gotta test it--are you still an impulsive, fiery nutcake?

Finally in safe circumstances you have massive PTSD. Bad memories, insults, horrifying treacheries.

Forget the lessons in the pits living in a ghost town--It's heaven when alone but invaders = black cloud.

Tho' without a fence and locked gate living in a ghosttown was great most the time 'til invaded by mob.

No longer alone in my desert oasis, women would invade and pick fights/seek to compete with me.

There is no house big enough for two women. And some are hyper-competitive, even pugnacious, vermin.

HOW TO WAIT

I know you invaders (names) and your collaborators. You wouldn't leave me alone and were such bores.

You were so jealous and envious that I was never bored or lonely, that I had no desire to be with thee.

YOUR WEAKNESS ATTRACTED EM

Don't blame them if your weakness was a magnet to their bad behavior--and that's how it works I swear.

Liberals wanna force people on you. Open borders, open doors: it's like it's illegal to have solitude.

Your kids wanna force their friends on you--only the strongest have a defense against this social undertow.

Liberals don't understand borders because they've been taught to be social in a constant party of horrors.

I was made to welcome pre-convicts in my house by a virtue-signaling Baptist lady saying how nice I was.

It's hard to believe those little creeps are in their fifties now but come to think of it most are immature anyhow.

They actually think they're intellectual for being liberal or democrat. They are hypnotized, that's a fact.

Liberals see the migrant flood as a great big party with Margaritas and guacamole, dear God!

Why don't you have a say in who your kid brings home? Are you kidding me, and in a locked room?

Only five cops in my tiny town, only five hours a day. The boys knew that and invaded me constantly.

I will never cease feeling invaded. Tho' I'm in safety now, INVASION leaves you with PTSD, jaded, tainted.

HOW TO WAIT

I figure I went thru it for a reason. To talk about invasion, open borders, the catastrophe that's facing us.

Parents no right to vet kid's friends? (That makes them haters?) Only the strongest have good defense.

My biggest life's lesson: It is near impossible for a female writer to work alone without interruption.

PEOPLE CAN BE DOWNERS

Tho' without a fence/locked gate living in a ghosttown was great most the time 'til invaded by bad fate.

When you came around my beautiful rainbow became a dark cloud of hurt feelings, feeling outcast/odd.

So good riddance, I've worked thru my PTSD of remembering all the evil things you did to me. I'm free.

I don't care whether you like me or not. That's not what it's about, a female writer must express self.

They couldn't stand it that I wanted solitude--minus them! Or they wanted solitude then bring all of em.

They wrote me off for choosing total solitude and I didn't give a dam! It was a test of loyalty to the clan.

I can't express how mean people are to those who want to be alone. Even churches attacked the crone.

I'm passed all that now, God put me in safety and a nice home. But that's when you get PTSD ya see?

Must let all this go now, get ready (clear the way, make a space) for the RIGHT PERSON to make the ace.

They'll get together and work each up into a mob then attack the lonely one who just wants to be alone.

HOW TO WAIT

The church ladies were the most jealous of my solitude. They'd get together and attack, gossip, ridicule.

False foods build a body filled with protuberances. All those bumps are cuz the poisons are sequestered.

Cortez is even more gesticulatory, loud, angry, and outlandish than ever and no one takes it for serious.

WHOOPI: the female community is always huggin' and kissin' and it makes me sick. YUK. hypocrites!

OBESITY AND DEATH FROM WALMART'S BAKERY

Bakery has always been flour-dairy-fruit but no more, it's all chemicals causing great pain: ACUTE!

Traditional bakery is flour, dairy and fruit. It was even good for you but now no more as chemicals pollute.

It tastes just like an eclair, a bear claw or a Danish! But it's not you fools it's all chemicals/not painless.

Vegans are like a stick, gonna have to give all that up I guess. Now I have hips but hubby says it's mint.

Protuberance, like humps on a camel. Oh I guess they aren't that bad it's just very novel, a real marvel.

All the cutsie ladies of the fifties had hips but tiny waists, a curvaceous symbol of the higher female caste.

The adolescent boy somatype just isn't reality for a lady. She has hips for example, showing dignity.

Sometimes eat every 36 hours, sometimes 72. After this vaca you'll be asking: where do I go from here?

FAST TO BE HAPPY IN AN AGEIST SOCIETY

HOW TO WAIT

So you feasted. That gives you an excuse to fast--life is two-fisted. It always turns out better, more elastic.

When I feel like humps on a camel I just take it as a symbol to fast that day, always saying "hurray"

People bring up age too much in an ageist society. When they fail to find a flaw they pull the age card, see?

It's rude to ask someone his age in an ageist society where they are judged by it when it should be irrelevant.

But they do it all the time so elders just sequester. It's a time to let go of all you knew/not let em pester.

I ended up on fruit cuz it's the only food going thru as everything else gets stuck then I'm down on luck.

Hijab would sure be cumbersome and hot when all a lady wants to wear is shorts and tank tops.

The answer to all dieting is the continuous reversals between all diets. Enjoy life even if you fry it.

When feeling a truck in the gut it's easy to fast so just enjoy the fasting day after eating way too much.

CLOSE YOUR BORDERS FOR SUCCESS

Well, when is he gonna do it? Why is he waiting? He should send 20,000 soldiers & close the border.

Now those boys are in their fifties and have no idea how they tortured me, their early days lost to memory.

The mesomorphic couldn't care less that I was cerebrotonic, reclusive, introverted or hypersensitive.

They were forced into social conformity and told to have friends, I was a boomer with less of this I contend.

HOW TO WAIT

They acted like they owned me immediately, like being kidnapped suddenly--and I prayed Lord help me!

From this terrible experience with young boys I understood what the girls go through, just sex toys?

INVADED, OR DID YA LET EM ALL IN?

My "friend" drunkenly let em in one night for tacos. From then on I couldn't get rid of the wackos.

What I went thru in a small desert town without cops was a sad depressing thriller like a serial killer.

When a gang of young boys vandalized my home the police couldn't do anything due to the ACLU? Explain.

Cuz I was too scared to report attempted rape the cops did a drug sting and he spent 20 years in the clink.

It was just like the sensitive Blanche in Streetcar Named Desire imposed on by her viscerotonic tormentor.

What is the effect on mothers putting up with these kids? Mal-adaptation to chaos/seared consciences.

Biggest mal-adaptation of parents to kids is addictions of all kinds or that sexual immorality blinds us.

An emaculate housekeeper and conscious cook for her family gives this up and fails into drugs or an alki.

A sharp dresser loses interest in exactitude or attention to detail and becomes sloppy--from mal-adapting.

A sweet caring lady becomes nervous, bristly, bitchy cuz they invaded her with expectations to be nasty.

CONTAGION OF LUNACY

HOW TO WAIT

The contagion of lunacy is when you give up in **EXHAUSTION** and become part of the problem, amen.

Gives up in exhaustion dealing with mixed signals, contradictions and status-tension and aggression.

When that exhausted and discouraged what do you have left? Delicious sins to comfort you with solace.

When that exhausted there is moral degradation. One gives up in maintaining LINES for a nice home.

No one would help me so I just lost my mind instead. I was really out there or exhausted in bed.

They thought I was crazy not exhausted from the false social--to complain of that you were hated double.

Across the nation parents are going thru hell. Each generation is different but this break is bombshell.

While you wait, think on these things. I'll bet you had obstructions like above keeping you waiting.

Before anything can happen for you, remove strife and bring aristocratic order to your essential homelife.

Once cleared of obstructions

HOW TO WAIT

you're just one good break away.

SOME FRUIT AND A BOWL OF RICE A DAY

If the most beautiful women in the world are men, why can't just any female be beautiful then?

A couple mangos and a bowl of rice a day. Hey--I live like the poorest in India and that's kinda cool, ok?

I can adapt in a shortage cuz rice and sugar is cheap and I bought a heap--it's a feather in my cap, see?

For dog breaks I take walks around the property and it looks magnificent like a painting or storybook.

Meat: I liked it as a child but mentally you change with the years and that determines your taste for sure.

I love my rice with fruit and a few nuts in it. With miso too the juxtaposition of flavors is mint/I'm lovin' it.

I woke up in a panic my heart racing, feared an attack then had some fruit and it all evened out, I'm back.

We gotta eat, right? So it's important we get that straight then it'll ALL be ok. Fruit and rice/spuds if you like.

I panicked and my heart raced, I thought it was all over. Then I took some fruit and got closure.

He's finally accepted I'm afraid of cars so to do errands alone. Wow, to spend 100% of time in home

HOW TO WAIT

THE END THOUGHTS

Parody exaggerates what's already there. If you're bad God won't anoint as you're common/not rare.

To the GIANT men of Utah: You changed my tire on the freeway twice, I know I'm in the right place.

These are self-evident truths, called "tautologies". But they go against the grain so bring insight.

Do all work to please yourself cuz the minute you do it for them it'll be dull and dry: no magic elf.

All I know is something triggers and you cry for a day. This starts the new life of riches I say.

Stop worthless accomplishments. Never produce until your mature or suffer embarrassment.

HOW TO WAIT

LIKE A CHRISTMAS GIFT:
CURE FOR LOSERS: BECOME FASTERS

Any goat, cow, lizard, cat or dog can do it. Does that make you some great player? No, GROW UP!

It's been a great regimen I will continue for life: Fast every weekend 60 hours from Fri 6 pm to Mon 6 am.

It's a self-cleaning body so if we don't eat, 85% of our energy [for digestion] goes to detox instantly.

If you must take something, a little yellow fruit juice auto-digests the gut residue: lemon or pineapple.

From Friday pm to Monday am: fasting is easy and seen correctly it's a exhilarating/adventurous reality.

I have so much energy on my weekend fasts I generally tear into housecleaning, ordering closets, projects.

I figured I was never hungry anyway and besides cooking is a chore, so why not fast? Found time, galore.

It's like encephalization is the reward for enduring hunger pain. It just lasts a minute before giant gains.

Started my fast 4pm Friday then worked all night long ordering a huge basement without sleep, ok?

You just gotta say: I WILL endure hunger pain, it ain't no big thing, it's no sweat, I'm higher than that.

EATING BECOMES IRRELEVANT/A CHORE

You will reach an age where eating is irrelevant to you, even the good stuff cuz digestive pain is rough.

I don't like it, I'd rather be high as a kite with ALL THAT ENERGY now going to my higher poetic mind.

100 KAREN KELLOCK BOOKS

AFFINITY OR MISERY
AGELESS CORNUCOPIA
AMERICA AWAKE!
AMERICA'S DAFT ERA
ARTS OF PALEO FASTING
AUTOPHAGY ON CHEATERS
BACKSTABBING NEUROTICS
BETRAYAL TRAUMA
BOOMERS AND BROKENNESS
BOOT ON NECK
CHAMPION GUIDES
COMMIE NUTHOUSE
COMMIES
COMMUNIST SPIRIT
CONTAGION OF MADNESS
CONTAGIOUS MADNESS
CULTURE CLASH BASHED
DAFT LEFT
DAILY FASTARIAN
DAM RATS
DIVERSITY IS CRUELTY
E-RACE WHITE
EVIL FREAKS (Beyond Gross)
THE END OR A BEND?
FEMALE BULLIES AND FEMI-NAZIS
FEMALE CARNALITY
FEMALE DUMB DOWN
FEMALE POWER DRIVE
FEMINISM AND RUIN 1 & 2
FIX FOR MISFITS
FOOLS & TRAMPS
FREEDOM SPEAKING
FRENEMY ENABLER
FRENEMY LIAR
FRENEMY THIEF
FRENEMY TRAITOR
TRENEMY TYRANT
GENIUS IS HELD DOWN
GLOBALISLAM
GOD USES THE FLAWED
HAZE OF THE LATTER DAYS

KAREN KELLOCK PH.D.

M.S. Political Science, San Diego State. Ph.D. in Psychology, University of California Irvine. Postdoctoral: UCI School of Medicine, Dept. of Psychiatry [NIMH Grants]. Developed the Debris Theory of Disease, a theory of system pathology in 120 books and 22 textbooks for the general public. The theory has a general formula: All disease is obstruction, all recovery is elimination, all success is attraction. The three obstructions are people, habit and food. Remove obstruction and snap to your goals, waiting in the wings.